P O E M S

CAMBRIDGE
UNIVERSITY PRESS

University Printing House, Cambridge CB2 8BS, United Kingdom

Cambridge University Press is part of the University of Cambridge.

It furthers the University's mission by disseminating knowledge in the pursuit of education, learning and research at the highest international levels of excellence.

www.cambridge.org
Information on this title: www.cambridge.org/9781107586178

First published 1919
First paperback edition 2015

A catalogue record for this publication is available from the British Library

ISBN 978-1-107-58617-8 Paperback

Donald F. Goold Johnson

POEMS

BY

DONALD F. GOOLD JOHNSON

WITH A PREFATORY NOTE BY

P. GILES, Litt.D.,
Master of Emmanuel College, Cambridge

CAMBRIDGE
AT THE UNIVERSITY PRESS
1919

PREFACE

THE poems in this book are all that remains of one who had hardly begun his work in literature when he had to leave it for the grimmer tasks of the European war. Many of the poems included here were written at the front, some even in the trenches on the battlefield whence the author did not return. Hence there are no doubt some things in these verses which the author, if he had lived longer, would have liked to alter. But there is little either in matter or in manner which he would have been forced to change.

Donald Fredric Goold Johnson was a son of the Manse. Born on March 6th, 1890, he received his school education from twelve to seventeen at Caterham. His home was at Saffron Walden and it is perhaps not too fanciful to detect in his love for describing quiet rural scenes with streams and woodland the influence of the landscape which he knew most intimately, even though the scene professes to be laid in Thessaly or some other classical land which, except in imagination, he was never destined to see.

As he was the youngest of four brothers it was necessary that he should be a teacher for some years before he could proceed to the University. In 1911 he came into residence at Cambridge, having been elected to a sizarship at Emmanuel College, and read for the Historical Tripos during his first two years. He was musical and was soon elected to a Choral Scholarship. Modest as to his own abilities at first he did not talk much or take any conspicuous part in College life. But by and bye he became better known, spoke at the Union, and took an increasingly important place in College societies. After Part I of the Historical Tripos he elected to read for the English section of the Medieval and Modern Languages Tripos. He was not a good examination candidate, though his teachers were sure that he had the root of the matter in him. Literature to him was a part of life, not knowledge to be pursued for gain. But though he took only a low place in the Tripos, he won the Chancellor's Medal for English Verse in 1914. Captain Scott's expedition was then much in men's minds and the poem is that headed *The Southern Pole.*

Johnson wished to make a special study of the text of Chaucer in the year after he graduated and to investigate carefully some of the less well-known manuscripts; and for this purpose his College provided him with the necessary means. But the war was at hand. By the end of the year it was clear to him that the country needed his help and he joined up. Soon he was posted to the Manchester Regiment and in the end of 1915 he went to France. He had previously joined the Roman Catholic Church, and so some of the poems show perhaps a clearer understanding than is common of the point of view of the village priest behind the lines and of his congregation. Ever susceptible to the beauty of the quiet countryside, Johnson delighted in the little French villages in which he found himself while he was still far behind the battle line.

In the struggle of 1916 he played his part as a brave soldier and a gallant officer. A trench had to be held at all costs and the Germans prevented from advancing. Johnson without hesitation undertook the task but bade his friends good-bye, fully certain that he should not return.

'First the blade, then the ear, after that the full corn in the ear.' What harvest Donald Johnson might have reaped in the fulness of time no man can tell; only a tiny sheaf of the firstfruits remains. And yet from this the reader may augur what the full grain would have been.

P. GILES.

11 *April* 1919.

[illegible]

[illegible] of [illegible] [illegible] [illegible] [illegible], standing them in common [illegible] [illegible] village [illegible] and the [illegible] [illegible] susceptibility to the [illegible] [illegible] side, [illegible] delighted [illegible] French [illegible] in which he [illegible] [illegible] ill [illegible] befitted to [illegible].

In the struggle of 1914 he played his part as a brave soldier and a gallant officer. A trench had to be held at all costs and the Germans prevented from advancing [illegible] without hesitation [illegible] took the [illegible] [illegible] [illegible] [illegible] fully [illegible] that he should not return.

[illegible] the blade [illegible] [illegible] that the full [illegible] [illegible] Donald Johnson [illegible] [illegible] the fulness of time [illegible] [illegible] only a tiny sheaf of the first [illegible]. And yet from this the reader may [illegible] what the [illegible] would have been.

[illegible] [illegible]

[illegible] April [illegible]

CONTENTS

Poems written during the War

1914–1916

Earlier Poems

MOTHER AND SONS

(*Cambridge, Easter Term, 1915*)

WE who have loved thee in days long over,
  Mistress immortal and Queen of our hearts;
With the passionate strength of a youthful lover,
  Take, ere for ever the glow departs,
Ere the flaming glead of our heart's devotion
  Flicker and fail as the night blows chill,
The homage that stirs no mock emotion
  'Tis thine, our Mother, to claim it still.

Dear to remember, the high June weather!
  (Soft thro' the shadows the boat glides on),
Rich are the dreams we have gathered together
  From the long hours of rapturous sun:
Tho' now with echoes of warfare sounding,
  Thy groves remember the cries of old;
And still, with their distant peace surrounding,
  Thy sons to thy bosom those arms enfold.

Then whether the sharp death face us daily,
  Thy youthful warriors lov'd of thee,
Thy tow'rs and palaces smiling gaily,
  In vision, our wishful eyes may see:
For all the hours of life and pleasure,
  For all the beauty by thee made known,
We pay thee in no stinted measure,
  But gladly lay our young lives down.

RESURGIT

THEY said that strength had passed from off the earth
With the last blazon of dead Chivalry;
That Faith had dipped its lance to Revelry,
And God been banished to the strains of mirth.
I think not that the blood of them that die
Lifts to the stars an empty sacrifice,
That prayers but batter a closed Paradise,
That heaven can answer not the hearts that cry
Upward for comfort; clearer now there ring
The song of faith triumphant over death,
The sound of praises thro' a mist of tears:
And not in vain they make their offering
Who, spent and shattered, clutch their dying breath;
Behold, the Son of Manhood reappears!

SPRING, 1915

LOOK long on the last lilac ere it fade;
  So soon it dies; and when it flowers again
Thy body in the still earth will be laid,
  Asleep to memory, and numb to pain;
Deaf to earth's music; and for thee no more
  The crocus-shower'd laburnum shall awake,
  And to the dawn its dancing tresses shake—
Tresses more radiant than Apollo wore.
Next year these shall renew their youth, but thou
  No more may'st look upon the bursting flow'rs,
    Nor daze thy senses with the breaths of Spring:
  Silent thou'lt lie throughout the endless hours;
    And all the pangs of earth's awakening
Shall not uncalm the stillness of thy brow.

RUPERT BROOKE

O WHAT fair death could greet him fairer yet
  Than to be gathered where the sweet sea smiles
  Lapping so tenderly the Grecian isles?—
Too sad for speech: too beauteous for regret—
His mother, England, shall not soon forget
  Her youngest singer, lovely as the sea:
  Within the glades of her deep memory
His name, his love, his glory she shall set.
The flowers are waking in her quiet fields,
  The woods are robing for their festival,
    By hedge and stream again the dear birds sing:
And all the beauty that the fresh earth yields,
  And all the springtime's maiden coronal.
    Shall be to him a silent offering.

JUSTITIA VICTRIX

'England shall ne'er be poor if England strive
Rather by virtue than by wealth to thrive.'
DEKKER'S *Old Fortunatus*, v. 2.

'SEE how my brave English fight!'
So our last Stuart spake, that day
When on the battle's issue lay
His claim to rule of sacred right.

Yea, tho' he faced an English foe
Whose gain would mean a fallen crown,
Not this might keep the triumph down,
Nor could his blood its pride forgo.

Two hundred years have passed anon
Since in Saint Germain's gloomy pile,
'Mid empty pomp of royal style,
His soul unto its King is gone.

To-day those hostile banners fly
Blown by one breeze and side by side,
One common purpose flames the pride
For which their warriors strike and die.

And still the claim of heavenly right
Flaunts o'er the armies of their foe,
To cover up a traitor's blow,
To mask the wounds of hell's despite.

We mock not thus the Lord of Hosts,
Make Him a vassal to our praise,
Nor echo in earth's stricken ways
Demonic taunts and godless boasts.

Not thus self-satisfied we stand
To face the lords of lust and blood,
But as in ancient days we stood
With Freedom's banner in our hand.

Strong in the panoply of Truth
With iron will we take the field,
Justice our Captain, Faith the Shield
Girding the flower of Britain's youth.

On Belgian fields the slaughter'd dead
Cry out with louder voices now
That their dear land shall never bow
To Tyranny her laurell'd head.

Low lie the victims on the plain,
And smoulder'd cities echo still
Their tale of woe from hill to hill:
No hand can e'er restore again.

Their mighty works of skill and grace—
Tow'rs, halls and temples which the dead
Had reared, and Time had garlanded
With beauty none can now replace.

March! march! brave comrades, march again!
Strike still to crush the vandal horde,
Till Justice bid you sheathe the sword,
And Victory stay your blood and pain.

Till beautiful the flow'rs of peace
Break from their buds so long up-seal'd,
Till Truth shall triumph in the field,
And all the red contention cease.

And they whose bones for ever lie
Deep in that earth whose face grew red
With the brave blood these heroes shed—
Can human hearts more nobly die?

Praise is no idle gift, the praise
Of lands and races that their might
Frees from the menace and the blight
Of feckless woes and servile days.

Their glorious names shall be adored;
Great was their love and great their worth;
Their fame shall purify the earth,
And Honour be their dear reward.

CHARLES LAMB

THERE are who win on tented fields the prize
Of glory, and achieve a moon of fame:
By fearless deeds these consecrate a name,
Gaining an added grace in Beauty's eyes.
And some there are for whom stern duty lies
In paths obscure, lit by no perilous flame;
Whose simple worth no plauding lips proclaim,
Nor voice of after ages glorifies.
Thy path was humble, and thy load of care
No fancied burden lightly to appraise;
Yet while Fame lives thy memory shall remain!
Rich was thy store of wit and genius rare,
And great shall be the harvest of the days
Ere kindlier heart than thine can beat again.

VICTOR VICTIMA

O SOV'REIGN Body broken on the tree,
  Mine is the traitor kiss that hangs Thee there:
  Yea, and the garden of Thy pale despair
    My heart's Gethsemane,

That garden where, upon the darkling sward
  Drunk with the greed of hell, the wage of death,
  Stealing upon Thee, with her treacherous breath
    My soul betrays her Lord.

Lo! mine the anguish of Thy piercéd side,
  My malice is that spear that woundeth Thee;
  Yet for Thy recreant lover, Lord, for me,
    In silence Thou hast died.

Still move Thy gentle lips to love and rue,
  While round Thee mock the children of Thy pain,
  'Forgive them, Father, for their hearts' disdain,
    They know not what they do.'

Breathe now, dear Jesus, as Thy darkness falls
  The peace no terrors quench, no pains dismay;
  Bring me, all-crucified, with Thee to-day
    Into Thy Father's halls.

ADVENT SONG

Jesu! sweet Fruit of that glad Tree
That God Himself did bless
With heavenly pure caress,
When Gabriel hailed with high decree
Our Lady full of grace,
Whose stainless heart Thyself didst fill;
Smile with Thy childish face
Free us from all peril.

Make Thou our hearts so to increase
In lowly purity,
That ever they may flee
The things that are not of Thy peace;
But Thou our spirits sway
With Thy dear love that may control,
Each hour of night or day,
Our wantonness of soul.

Guard us, dear Saviour, with Thy hand
That piercéd was for us;
So, led and fostered thus,
We find at last Thy pleasant land,
Where, purged and purified,
We too may dwell within Thy bow'rs
With all the sanctified
Thro' the eternal hours.

H. M. J.

(Died July 24th, 1915)

God fashions for the hearts of men
To love, rare souls whose radiant light
Thrills like a meteor thro' our ken
Streaking the greyness of the night.

Not theirs the slow long-numbered years
That smoulder without heat or flame;
With fiercer joys and sadder tears
These weave a glory for their name.

Such light was hers, whom Beauty lent
So sweet a temple for the soul;
Freely for others it was spent,
Till, deepening, the shadows stole.

There where beneath the Indian sky,
By banks the Ganges' waters lave,
Among the swampy rice-fields lie
The homes of them she lived to save.

Youth, beauty, charm, and strength and health—
She laid them at the feet of Love,
Gaining a far diviner wealth
That pain and death could not remove.

After her labour and her pain
She tastes the fountains of delight,
Counting her human loss but gain:
The handmaid in her Master's sight.

YOUTH AND WAR

Among the windy spaces
  The star-buds grow to light;
With pale and weeping faces
  The day-hours bow to night;
Where down the gusty valleys
  A blast of thunder dies,
And in the forest alleys
  A startled night-bird cries.

Not pain but bitter pleasure
  Surrounds my spirit here,
For life's supernal treasure
  Is garlanded with fear;
Bright trees delight the garden
  About my love's glad home,
But all the flower-roots harden
  Under the frost of doom.

Like the bright stars above me
  My youthful hopes were set!
Yearning for lips that love me;
  O how can I forget
The boyish dreams that brought me
  To the high azure gate
Of heaven, where beauty sought me,
  And love was satiate?

Now honour lets me dally
  No longer with desire,
But goads me to the valley
  Of death, and pain, and fire;
Not love but hate constraining
  The soldier in the field,
Honour alone remaining
  Of virtue for a shield.

Yet who dare doubt, resigning
  The joys that mortals prize—
Beyond the heart's repining,
  Behind the sightless eyes—
For all the tears and anguish,
  The piteous dismay—
True love at length shall vanquish,
  And crown the dawning day?

LES PAUVRES MORTS

At evening thro' the garden ground I strayed
  Among the peasant graves of years gone by,
Where now too many of our youth are laid,
  The dear, dead flowers of English soldiery;
And there an ancient village dame who prayed
  And wept for that strange-harbour'd argosy
I saw, beside a row of mounds new made,
  Sobbing her mother's heart so piteously.
Not for her own she wept; for she could care
  For their quiet heritage from day to day;
But for the mothers whose sad hearths are bare,
  Whose poor dear sons find rest so far away
From home and England and their Mother's tears,
To sleep so lonely through the silent years.

ODE ON THE RESURRECTION

Out from the womb of Time,
  The young day came to birth,
Startling with praise sublime
  The silence of the earth;
Till all the skies around
Trembled to shimmering light and soft harmonious sound.

This is the day designed
  Thro' all the tale of years,
When He whom death confined
  In triumph reappears,
To claim His glorious crown,
Hell vanquished, and the might of Satan beaten down.

Where pale light crowns the hills
  With the first flush of dawn,
Whose gradual bounty fills
  The spaces of the morn,
Against the eastern skies
One awful picture greets the fearful watchers' eyes.

Above dark Calvary
  A lonely rood-tree shows
Its hateful imagery,
  Its panoply of woes:
And there the Lord of Love did die;
O bitter were the tears of Mary standing by!

How tenderly they bare
  That Body from the tree,
With looks of wan despair,
  And speechless misery;
To the cool garden cave
Whose depths should serve the King of Glory for a grave.

How lovingly they dressed
  The wounds that Love had borne;
How reverently caressed
  Those features so forlorn;
Smoothed back the tussled hair,
Anointing each pale limb with oils and spices rare.

The guardian tomb was sealed
  With the Imperial sign,
But breaking day revealed
  No shackles might confine,
Nor watch nor ward restrain
The Prince of Life who rose to glorious life again.

When early in the morn
  Of that expected day
Ere the first light was born
  On dim hills far away,
Those two disciples came
Breathing in hopeless hope that sorrow-shrouded name,

O what celestial sight
Struck their sad murmurs dumb,
Of angels radiant bright
Guarding an empty tomb?
(No silent body there,
Only the linen clothes of costly texture fair.)

'What seek ye here?' they cry,
'Have ye so soon forgot?
Behold The Day is nigh,
Give praise and sorrow not;
Your Master, risen indeed,
Goeth to Galilee; speed ye where He doth lead.'

As sadly they had come,
O'erborne with doubt and fear,
Thro' the cool garden gloom
To that dark sepulchre,
Now each heart leaps and thrills
With wild delight, and song each soul exultant fills.

The dull relentless skies
Break into hues of dawn,
The sleepy flowers arise
And curtsy to the morn,
Where thro' the garden way
The cluster'd dew lies fresh, catching the fires of day

And one alone who came—
  Ere the first morning glow
Had sparkled into flame—
  In bitterness of woe;
And doubtingly espied
Before the cavernous tomb the great stone rolled aside:

As she with breaking day
  Thro' the wet garden fares,
She meets upon her way
  Her Master unawares,
And questions Him if He
Can tell her where the body of her Lord may be.

Then He in answer sweet
  That puts to flight her fear
Doth her, all-wond'ring, greet,
  And make His presence clear:
'Mary'—He saith, and she—
'Master' amazed replies, and bendeth low the knee.

'Arise, arise, Mary,
  And love shall be your speed,
Tell them that mourn for me
  Their Lord is risen indeed'—
Heaven's purpose is fulfilled,
Death may no longer keep the God whom sin had killed.

'Twas thus the Prince of Love
  From rueful death did rise,
And bore His wounded shape
  Immort to Paradise;
Where now He stays in bliss,
Till every soul that is
Endued with mortal flesh
  No more shall seek the bitterness of sin,
  But, clarified within,
May potent rise and break the fowler's mesh.
Then when the souls made true
  Do seek the heavenly floor,
And Michael with his fiery sword
  Guarding the flaming door
Doth those proud gates unfurl,
  That gracious Prince of Love shall stand,
Gold-rob'd, and crown'd with diadems of pearl;
  And stretching wide each wounded hand,
Shall greet with smiling face
Each soul to that dear place.

REIMS

THY altars smoulder, yet if Europe's tears
 Can stay the doom of malice, they are thine
 To quench the fires that lick thy sacred shrine,
And scar the treasures of thy glorious years.
Yet nought can salve the heart's despairing fears
 That knows its Head dishonour'd, while rapine
 Thunders upon His citadel divine,
Till all its ancient splendour disappears.
But courage! tho' no hand can raise again
 Thy perish'd glories, garlanded by Time,
 The arm yet faileth not that ruleth all!
And God Himself the guilty shall arraign,
 Bidding them answer their inhuman crime
 Before His everlasting doom shall fall.

LOVE IN WAR

O FOR your mouth's vermilion stain,
  To watch and love thro' night and day,
To sip and taste and drink again,
Fragrant as gardens after rain
    On golden nights of May!

I long to steep my eager sight
  In your young limbs' deliciousness,
Their naked beauty, soft and white,
Yielding its grace for my delight,
    To cure my vain distress.

But lips to crush and limbs to bind
  In silent rapture of desire—
Youth's crowning joys—I've left behind:
Yet who to death would be resigned
    Whose heart love sets afire?

When life is free and fighting's done,
  Will love be sweeter than before?
(Hope will not think of you left lone),
But when the crowning triumph's won
    Will ever peace restore

Those precious dreams that silent came
  To soothe my troubled sleep at night?
Will love burn with as fierce a flame,
And only to repeat your name
    Bring as secure delight?

L'INCONNUE

I WHO have lived for beauty
  And found strange comfort so,
Since love is all my duty
  O what can I bestow
Save love, unsought, unheeded,
As incense for your grace,
  A gift of adoration
    For love's dear face.

Thro' spring-time dawns of singing,
  In sunset flowers of flame,
I hear for ever ringing
  The wonder of your name,
The magic charm that bears me
  Behind the fires of dawn,
Beyond the sunset silence,
    All love-forlorn.

Tho' other lips shall kiss you
  And quaff my wine of love,
Shall savour the soft tissue
  Of lips the fairies wove;
Tho' round your fragrant body
  Twine limbs of living fire,
They will not know the passion
    Of my desire.

Pure as the crystal beaker
 That but reflects the wine,
Your spirit is the liquor
 With which those bright eyes shine;
With half the world to flatter,
 And all the world to praise,
Unspoiled, you taste the rapture,
  Of youthful days.

O gay light-hearted singer
 Whose song no tremor shows
That death with chilly finger
 Lurks in the shadows close;
Wise, you refuse to hearken
 For whispers of his call;
But oh, the heavens would darken
  If Love should fall!

Ah many are the faces
 That I have fairest found,
In strange and distant places
 I've sought the long world round;
Yours now, the last and rarest,
 Of beauty's grace the crown,
The gayest and the fairest,
  I love unknown.

BATTLE HYMN

Lord God of battle and of pain,
  Of triumph and defeat,
Our human pride, our strength's disdain
  Judge from Thy mercy-seat;
Turn Thou our blows of bitter death
  To Thine appointed end;
Open our eyes to see beneath
  Each honest foe a friend.

Give us to fight with banners bright
  And flaming swords of faith;
We pray Thee to maintain Thy right
  In face of hell and death.
Smile Thou upon our arms, and bless
  Our colours in the field,
Add Thou, to righteous aims, success
  With peace and mercy seal'd.

Father and Lord of friend and foe
  All-seeing and all-wise,
Thy balm to dying hearts bestow,
  Thy sight to sightless eyes;
To the dear dead give life, where pain
  And death no more dismay,
Where, amid Love's long terrorless Reign,
  All tears are wiped away.

JUNE

Sweet month of love and roses, hail!
Queen of all joys that never fail;
  The grasping fingers of fern are open,
The may still blossoms adown the vale.

And all thy bevy of maiden flow'rs
Blush and bloom thro' the golden hours,
  Where pink, full-blown rhododendron bushes
Make on the green lawn fairy bow'rs.

Softly thy ev'ning sunbeams play,
Thine are the iris nights that are day,
  Thine are the love-born hearts that blossom,
Kissing the languorous hours away.

O June, Queen June, thy reign is here!
In the palace of days thou hast never a peer;
  For the voices of bird-throats richly mellow
Hail thee as Queen of the garland year.

COMBIEN APRÈS?

It may be, in the after-years,
  Our souls shall touch across the space,
It may be, on my heart of tears
  Shall break the music of thy grace;
But who can make again for me
That perfect form, that maddening glee?

It may be that thy voice shall speak
  Across a universe unknown,
Like some gold-flecker'd sunset streak
  That crowns one moment's bliss alone;
But shall I know in Paradise
Thy godly lips and hands and eyes?

It may be, in that heavenly land
  All priests and prophets have foretold,
That spectre beings hand in hand
  The great white throne of God enfold;
But shall I *feel* and *see* thee there,
And kiss the flowers of thy hair?

It may be, Sweet, that love shall live
  Beyond the shadow-hours of Death,
That Hope some comfort still shall give
  When this fond body yields its breath;
But could I know that I should see
Thy glorious lips, all fear would flee.

It may be, in another world
   Far from the sorrowings of this,
I still shall watch thy lips shy-curl'd
   And taste their beauty in a kiss;
It *may* be—but the very *may*
Takes half the glorious hope away.

Then, Darling, kiss me while the light
   Shines on thy hair and radiant form,
This day at least the sun is bright
   And bodes no darkness of the storm;
Come, let us join our sweet lips fast
Tho' this same hour should be our last.

SUNT LACRIMAE RERUM

O to think that Beauty liveth
  Such a little while,
All the sweets of joy it giveth,
  Kiss and glance and smile,
Fading like the fallen day,
Dying evermore away.

O to think that Love can ever
  Feel the ice of Death,
That the earth it spurns can sever
  Mingling lips and breath;
Cold and sad it lieth still,
Once so glowing, now so chill.

O to think that Thou my fairest
  Far away shall fly,
And the angel form thou wearest
  Droop to earth and die;
O what joy can overweigh
Such deep burdens of dismay?

O to think that Beauty dieth
  Like a thing of dross,
Broken in the grave-way lieth
  Under leaf and moss,
All its passion and delight
Quench'd amid the voiceless night.

A VISION

As down from out the flaming quire,
  The white-cloth'd singers pass'd,
And from the carven organ's throat
  Echo'd a trumpet blast,

I saw thy winsome, graceful form
  Thread the slow-pacing throng,
And turn to climb the ancient stair,
  My sweet-mouth'd child of song.

And then into my heart there came
  A strange and sudden glee:
I saw an angel pass to heav'n,
  And thou thyself wert he.

ST DYMAS

Hot was the noon and weary was the road,
Dusty and spent the travellers thereon,
The Father walking by the ass's head
The Mother with her Son.

Down into Egypt fleeing from the wrath
Of the fierce king who fear'd a rival's birth
A lowly babe in Mary's arms He passed
Whose Name should rule the earth.

So faint and weary to a well-head came,
That tiny band of travellers at last,
And paused to rest until the heat of day
Should all be overpast.

A woman drawing water there they meet
Who smiles a kindly smile upon the Child,
Which sweetly He gives back, and turns in glee
Unto that Mother mild.

Then Mary to the village maiden spake:
'Give me, I pray thee, of thy water there,
For we are hot and parch'd and travel-sore
Under this burning air.'

Then gave the woman water in her bowl,
And Mary drank, and wash'd the babe, and spake
Sweet words of blessing to the peasant girl
Who gave, their thirst to slake.

Then they moved onward, while the woman stood
And watched them till the three had pass'd from sight;
When homewards gaily singing she did go,
A song of glad delight.

And took the self-same water in the bowl
Wherein the Holy Mother bath'd the Child,
For pure and clear and bright it sparkled still
A fountain undefil'd.

And plac'd therein her own poor leprous babe,
Dymas his name, and leprous from his birth:
Some said as penance for his sire's ill-fame,
A robber nothing worth.

And she, poor mother, laid him with a sigh
Of wondrous pitying love within the bowl;
A leper-babe she sprinkled, but drew out
A babe all cleans'd and whole.

NOX BENIGNA

Thro' the midst of the starlight you came to my soul
  To lie once again on my breast,
And dreams of thy rapturous loveliness stole
  Across the dark veil of my rest.

I saw thee, I touch'd thee, my arms did entwine
  Thy body of gossamer flesh,
I kissed thy soft hair, than spun silk-thread more fine,
  Thy lips than dew-roses more fresh.

I search'd thy deep eyes for the tale of thy love,
  Those eyes of so wondrous a hue,
For ne'er in the sea nor the star-space above
  Was seen so enchanted a blue.

I kiss'd thy clear cheek, thy soft neck, thy white hands,
  And mingled thy breath with my own,
I bound thy soft arms like sweet osier-bands
  To the breast where my passion is sown.

I awoke! and the night that was kindled with light
  Was turn'd to the darkness of day;
Thy body had pass'd from my touch and my sight,
  Thy beauty had vanish'd away.

O rapture of God that was mine for an hour,
  And taken as swiftly as giv'n,
O bring me again with my blossoming flow'r
  The bliss of the angels of heav'n.

THE RIVER-BRIDGE

THE sacred hour again! O silent years,
  Scarce may I feel how far Time's feet have run
Since this dear place I hallow'd first with tears.
  Still over lawn and meadow plays the sun,
As on that blessed even long ago
It deck'd my love and glorified my woe.

Here by this crumbling parapet I stood
  Beneath the drooping willow's veil of June,
Teaching my eyes to sound the dreamy flood
  Whose depths just mirror'd the awak'ning moon,
Like a pale spectral spirit of the sky
To mark how soon the golden hour must fly.

The golden hour! how could my heart foretell
  That this one heedless hour should shine alone?
Like some green isle where syren-voices dwell,
  With rose-strewn lawns and dreamy bowers sown,
Where Love and I might dwell for evermore
Nor heed the moaning breakers on the shore.

I knew not that the sun-bath'd hour should be
Like this enchanted bridge where yet I stand—
And then we stood—for all eternity
My stream of life flowing on either hand
Of that still hour, as here the river's flow
Beneath these spandrel'd arches deep doth go.

For Thou didst come, and there we two alone
Drank deep of heaven thro' our trembling eyes;
The tender lips I gazed on sought my own,
Rich-scented, luscious fruits of Paradise;
And thy white arms were mine to fondle there,
Thy godly beauty food for love's despair.

Few words were ours, for lips have better use
Than empty words to murmur, while our eyes
Sang ever each to each in songs profuse
Of passion's worship and love's high emprise;
Yet only for a moment my delight,
The gates of heaven clos'd as you pass'd from sight.

One long look back thou gavest that must feed
My hopeless longing through all future days,
Till light and life before death's self recede;
No more upon thy beryl eyes to gaze!
No more to sip the may-dew of thy mouth!
Thro' the long world to bear my quenchless drouth.

Yet, for slow years of ceaseless wandering
All up and down the pain-encumber'd earth,
One moment would suffice again to bring
Our dead but unforgot delight to birth;
One moment of thy presence, one dear smile
From thy sweet mouth, should pay this weary while.

O I shall find thee, tho' I know not where!
O I shall greet thee, tho' I know not when!
Kiss first the whispering fragrance of thy hair,
Thy shy pale face and tremulous hands, and then
On thy full lips' rich blossom stay my own,
Till mouth to mouth in one soft flow'r is grown.

MY LADY OF THE JOUST

(*XIV Century*)

LADY, my lance is bended low
Before thy flower-encircled brow,
With all my strength to praise thee, I
Ride forth to triumph or to die.

Where is the fame that tempts my pride?
In thy pure heart it doth abide;
My gage to honour thee is thrown,
To flaunt no favour but thine own.

Thyself the guerdon of my might,
Thy love is armour for the fight,
Thine is the cause, the victory,
Yea, all the praise is unto thee.

Fresh as snowdrop and aconite
When first in spring they break to sight,
Shall mocking lust pollute the breath
Those dear lips breathe, and not taste death?

Nay, I will triumph, and thy shame
Fling in the teeth where thro' it came:
Beauty and love must sure avail
To cause this devil's wiles to fail.

Then smile, dear lady, as I ride
Into the lists, to spur my pride:
My valour thus shall strike and win
To break this malison of sin.

Here is thy fillet, at my heart,
They two not Life nor Death shall part;
If by hell's spite I fall, thy tear
At least may grace thy lover's bier.

A MEMORY

Could I but see thy face again
  A moment's space,
Its young, delightful mock-disdain,
  Its wooing grace;
Could I but kiss thy wilful hair,
  That restless hand,
Would you divine how dear you were
  And understand?

Why was it when our hearts were near
  They would not speak?
What barrier of love's shy fear
  Could we not break?
When all my living was thy love
  My lips were dumb,
Only when chance and place remove
  The accents come.

In those sweet days my daily bread
  Was seeing thee;
Richly my heart with love was fed,
  And poesy.
Now others love where I have loved,
  And taste their fill,
So far away is that removed
  I worship still.

Now for the garden of thy lips
  I only sigh;
My sun of life dark clouds eclipse
  'Thwart all the sky;
O in thy new-won paradise
  Wilt thou recall
The love that found in thy young eyes
  The sum of all?

A WISH

LET me not pass through life's brief days
  Loving yet loved not with desire!
Keep not for me the shadowy ways
  Of indolent dreams, without real fire
    Of mutual love's amaze.

Let me not sing of others' joy,
  Nor shape my verse to imaged dreams
Of tender love 'twixt girl and boy,
  While from a lover's eyes no gleams
    My passionate eyes employ!

Let me not in pale thought alone
  Cherish the body of my bride;
But, living lips upon my own,
  In trembling joy be satisfied,
    Crown'd upon Love's high throne!

TO A SUNDIAL

SET IN AN OLD ENGLISH GARDEN

Still, silent, gentle reckoner of the hours
  That mark the never-pausing steps of Time,
  A visitor from some immortal clime
Thou seem'st, with tidings from the eternal pow'rs.
Autumn and spring, gay sunshine and soft show'rs,
  And summer's heat and winter's glistering rime
  Pass o'er thy brow, and morn and ev'ning chime
Make music for thee still among the flow'rs.
Thou know'st the charm of all the halcyon days,
  And youth and Love's soft pleasures, and hast seen
    Youth changed to Age, and Love to pale Regret.
Time casts its shadow o'er thy patient face
  And on man's joy, and all earth's royal sheen.
    Yet Man not Time shall triumph even yet.

'CHILD-FORM OF FLESH AND BLOOD'

Child-form of flesh and blood whose love outweighs
  All the world's ills, and makes the bare earth heaven;
  To thee these tribute songs of love are given:
Nought but a lover's coronal of praise,
Fresh budding blossom of the flowery days
  When love is young in perfect loveliness,
  And hearts know nought of sorrow or distress,
Nor all the sadness of the lonely ways.
Life is not all such gladness, tho' the heart
  Knows a far deeper meed of joy than pain,
    Pain that but heightens all the holy thrill
    Of beauty and of love that life doth fill,
  Like some dark tonic show'r of summer rain
That brighter leaves the sun when clouds depart.

THREE AGES

To-day I saw a picture of mankind
Set in the beauty of an autumn sky;
And while the sun lay softly on the woods
That mock'd its colour, and the querulous rooks
Flew slowly homeward o'er the sleepy fen,
I wove the human picture into song.

I. YOUTH

SINGING gaily in the meadows
Merrily as the dancing shadows,
  All the wealth of life is unto thee,
Shepherd Boy! whose smiles are dearer
Than the dawn; whose voice is clearer
  E'er than silver Pan-pipe's tune could be.

Nought of joy shouldst thou be missing;
Thy red lips are ripe for kissing,
  All of love lies at thy hand to-day;
Ne'er a girl so shyly pretty
But would love thy merry ditty,
  And the mouth that wove its tune so gay.

While the sun is bright around thee
Nought of sorrow can confound thee;
  Life is light, and youth is lithe and fleet.
Live thy song while life is tender,
Dream not that its thread is slender,
  Life for thee is gay, and beauty sweet.

II. MANHOOD

As I journey'd on I saw
One who drove his beasts before;
Soberly he trudged along,
From his lips there flowed no song.

But his steps were stiff and slow
Little joy had they to go,
And his pace was dull and set
Not with age but with regret.

Life had seemed so rich a thing
With his darling in the spring,
When in boyhood he had strayed
Wooing in the forest glade.

But he, as the years drop by,
Sees her beauty pale and die;
And their children ail and need,
Whom he scarce can clothe and feed.

So they die, and clouds obscure
Life that once was bright and pure;
Till he wonders in his toil
If its light be worth the oil.

III. AGE

Then in the simple beauty of a lane
Where silence steep'd my heart in balm again,
Leaning upon a gate, gazing away
Over the fields and woods that golden lay
Beneath the autumn sunlight, I espied
An aged man, deep-wrinkled and dim-eyed.
Motionless there he stood as if he grew
As the proud elms and nodding poplars do;
And tho' his face was aged, yet it wore
A long lost brightness it had known of yore—
Some echo of glad youth and wild surprise
That glimmer'd in his tender boyish eyes
When first his heart enkindled with love-fire
And lips and limbs were mingled in desire.
But now the joys of passion long are past,
His wearied limbs their labour fail at last.
And what of life remains when youth and love
With all their deeps of joy and grace remove?

After the heat and clangour of the day
Does all the glow and splendour die away
To leave the chill of night with no repay?
I see the mark of peace upon his face,
Of pensive quiet and a wintry grace,

The calm of lonely forest pools, the gleam
Of winter sunsets in still fields, that dream
Lull'd by the murmur of the flooded stream
Beneath a placid sky; and there is set
The sober joy that vanquishes regret
Upon his patient brow; and in his soul
The balm to make his wounded spirit whole.

THE GARDEN OF PEACE

HAIL, oh! hail to thee! Spirit of Quiet,
Child of the Muses, thy charms never cease.
Hail to thee! Hail to thee! Haven of Beauty,
Harbour of Solitude, Garden of Peace.

Far from the babbling in Cities of Tumult,
Far from the clashing of armies in strife,
Sweet-breathing, flower-strewn garden of England,
Ah! in thy shades is the wisdom of life.

Sweet are the breezes that breathe in thy flowers;
Soft come the voices of choristers here;
Softly and sweet from thy Chapel of Shadows
Pealings of Music, majestic and clear.

Many the hours of silence and pleasure
Spent in thy cloistral, familiar shades;
Oh! may their mem'ry ne'er leave me for ever,
Living when all but life's happiness fades.

Peace to thee! Peace to thee! arbour of melody,
Ne'er may the balm of thy solitude cease.
Neighbour'd and hallow'd by Temple of sanctity,
Sleep in thy loveliness, Garden of Peace!

PERSEPHONE

PROLOGUE

Boy. O FATHER, I am tir'd with play;
The night is hot, no breeze doth stir
Thro' the tall pine-tops on the hills
And all the boys are gone away
Back to their homes to cool themselves.
Thy work is done, come tell to me
Out here upon the cool hillside
As is thy wont on summer eves,
An ancient tale of Gods and men.

Father. The Gods are gracious,
The Gods are just;
From Olympus their dwelling,
The home of immortals,
They look upon all men
The Children of Earth.
The strong and the mighty,
The frail and the helpless,
The good and the godless,
They care for us all.
Nor least doth the Mother
Of fulness and plenty,
Demeter, sweet goddess
Of corn and of wine—
Of her will I tell thee,
Of her and her daughter
Fairest Persephone,

Queen of Immortals
Save Aphrodite
Goddess of Beauty
Of Beauty and Love.

'Twas summer in the fields of Sicily
Long, long ago when yet the earth was young.
And that fair footstool of proud Italy
Knew not, as yet, the poet's magic tongue;
Still were immortals seen by stream and glen,
Nor veil'd their faces from the eyes of men.

There came to those glad vales of summer sun
Demeter sweet, and fair Persephone,
The fairest of immortal maids save one
E'er mortal or immortal eye did see.
No necklet ever knew such radiant pearls
As that sweet maiden with her train of girls.

In Enna's fields at break of day they pass,
Thro' lily cups and ringing daffodils
And violets among the shining grass,
To cull the white narcissus from the hills.
Persephone with all her girlish train.
Alas! this way she ne'er shall pass again.

For far within his darksome realm below,
In murky climes that never know the sun,
Proud Hades sadly wanders to and fro;
Forth to the earth his wistful gazes run.
He sees its Princes gaily wed but he
For ever there in loneliness must be.

Since no immortal maid to be his bride
  Would leave the sunshine and the summer air,
For those sad shades where mortals that have died
  Make constant moan and wailing ever there.
Dark is the cloudy barrier that shields
That land from Heroes in Elysian fields.

There Hades reigns alone in sad complain
  That he alone must reign for evermore,
Till Hermes hears his solitary strain
  And speeds his flight to that forgotten shore—
Swift Hermes, winged messenger of heav'n,
By whom the edicts of the Gods are giv'n.

To him he tells the cause of all his woe,
  How love to him for ever is denied.
For no immortal girl would ever go
  To Erebus profound, his willing bride;
And mortal maiden could he never wed,
Nor seek a bride among the ghostly dead.

But Hermes bids him cheer his troubled breast
  And stem the tide of all his galling fears.
For gods have strength to aid a god's behest,
  And dry the fountain-heart of all his tears.
As thus he spake he cast his gaze above
To that sweet vision of immortal love.

Thro' garland glades their sweet way gaily wend
 Persephone and all her maiden band;
They sing a song of love that hath no end
 And pass the fresh-pull'd flowers from hand to hand.
These Hermes sees upgazing from below,
And doleful Hades from that land of woe.

'Behold a queen among immortal maids
 Sweet goddess blossom-ey'd Persephone,
Whose fairy foot thro' Enna's sunny glades
 Makes music in a flow'ry symphony.
No fairer wilt thou gain to be thy bride
Tho' thou shalt cross the world from side to side.'

Thus Hermes spake and straightway thence did fly
 Back to the gardens and the halls of heav'n;
And Hades watch'd his going, with a sigh
 Of blessing for the comfort he had giv'n.
Then turn'd again his gaze to earth above
And fill'd his spirit with the thoughts of love.

Then by his magic art he caused to grow
 Up from the bosom of the radiant earth,
Where that sweet goddess walk'd with footsteps slow,
 The fairest flower e'er beauty brought to birth;
A perfect narcissus of stainless hue
Full in her path was sudden brought to view.

For Narcissus was once a mortal boy
  Who lay beside the marge of a fair lake
And saw his image clear; with wond'ring joy
  He tried but fail'd to reach; and for its sake
He pin'd away with sorrow from that hour
And him the gods chang'd to a lovely flower.

She darted forward with a merry cry
  To pluck a bloom of loveliness so rare.
Alas! no guardian form was standing by,
  No heavenly warning shook the upper air!
And so in girlish innocence she took
The fateful flower, whereat the whole earth shook.

The earth was parted at her very feet,
  And forth a fiery chariot did spring
With horses wild, whose breath was burning heat
  And deadly vapour overpowering;
And Hades in the chariot did ride
And snatch'd the unwilling goddess to his side.

Then quick as he had come they disappear
  From the sad gaze of all her girlish train,
Who fill with bitter groans the callous air
  With lamentation deep and loud complain;
But sad Persephone with stifl'd breath
Is borne to darkness and the land of death.

Oh! loudly mourned Demeter for her child,
  Nor ever might her heart be comforted;
No longer to the silver morn she smiled,
  But with a dark cloak gather'd o'er her head
Nine days she wander'd all the world around,
Holding a flaming torch to scan the ground.

Yet still no traces of Persephone
  Her watchful eyes espied; but on the morn
Of the tenth day, the maiden Hecate
  She chanc'd to see among the golden corn:
Sweet Hecate, the maid of ankle rare,
If she might haply lighten her despair.

She had but seen the chariot to pass
  Nor knew or whence it came or whither fled,
But the great sun-god, fiery Helius,
  View'd all things from his flaming palace dread,
And he could tell her where her child was gone
And by whose hand the hateful deed was done.

Thus Hecate. Demeter forth doth wend
  Her sad way to the palace of the Sun,
If Helius might any comfort lend
  Or give her tidings of her truant one;
He in his lofty chariot is set
Where all the streaking flames of dawn are met.

He tells her all the melancholy tale:
  How it had been ordained of Father Zeus
Persephone to Erebus' dark pale
  Should be betrayed by Hades' cunning ruse;
And what great Zeus ordaineth it must be,
For he is Lord of Man and Deity.

Demeter sad forsook the halls of Heaven,
  Nor sweet ambrosia tasted any more,
But wander'd thro' the earth, her sad heart riv'n,
  Nor knew the gladness she had known before;
Thro' ways untrod by men and paths unknown
And silent wilderness she pass'd alone.

* * * * *

In golden Attica one sunny morn
  In sweet Eleusis 'neath a crystal sky
By a cool well Demeter sat forlorn
  And bitterly, oh bitterly did cry
For her lost child in Erebus' dim shade,
With weeping she did mourn and looks dismay'd.

Forth to the well-side came at early morn
  The daughters of the King of that bright land;
They see an ancient dame with look forlorn,
  But nought of her true race they understand,
For she had veiléd her divinity
In garb of eld and looks of misery.

Their pitchers fill'd they ask her to repair
   Unto their Father's home and there to rest,
For that the sun had scorch'd the parched air,
   And there she might find comfort for her breast.
Then gladly with them doth she leave the well
A season in that kindly home to dwell.

Now Celeus was the King of that brave land,
   And Metaneira was his gentle queen;
A fair-fac'd boy they had, of visage tann'd
   Where the fierce sun and blue sea's kiss had been,
A Prince in heart and limb and spirit mild,
And him the goddess lov'd as her own child.

Demophoön his name, and him she lov'd
   And sought to make immortal, but the fear
Of his own mother Metaneira prov'd
   A let to cause the goddess many a tear,
For, sleeping, she had plac'd him in the fire
With mutter'd charm and incantation dire.

But when those magic rites were all but done
   And all his mortal parts were purg'd away,
To that dread room the fearful queen did run
   And 'Lack a day!' she cried 'O lack a day!'
By mortal speech the awful spell was broke
And, mortal still, the hapless boy awoke.

Then all the earth was stricken for her woe,
  For ever did she mourn Persephone,
Nor corn, nor fruitful herb, nor flow'r did grow,
  Nor leafy veil put on a single tree;
But all the earth did mourn in visage sad
And sombre garb of death and winter clad.

Then had the race of mortals perish'd quite
  From off the earth and vanish'd utterly,
Yet Father Zeus had pity on their plight
  And hearken'd to their cry of misery,
And Hermes sent across the halcyon seas
If he the goddess' sorrow might appease.

He proffer'd all the glory, all the fame
  That to immortal soul could e'er be giv'n,
And wondrous wealth of riches in the name
  Of Zeus the Father and the King of Heaven,
Would she but cease to mourn and freely yield
Her balm of life again to grove and field.

But ever she in lonely misery
  With many a broken sigh and many a moan
Calls softly for her child Persephone;
  Not wealth nor fame she seeks, but her alone,
Her daughter, her sweet maid, her lily fair
With flow'ry eyes and flower-encircl'd hair.

So Zeus did promise her her child again,
  If she had tasted nought of food below;
Then lost the goddess all her mighty pain
  And dried her heart of all its tears of woe.
And Hermes cross'd again the sullen strand
That bounds the borders of that twilight land,

And bade proud Hades yield again his bride
  To the pure sunlight and the mellow air,
Who at the bidding of dread Zeus complied
  Tho' dearly did he love his lady fair,
And she at length had listen'd to his suit
And, parting, ate with him a pledge of fruit.

Then upwards to her mother's arms she sped;
  Yet for that she had tasted food below,
For half the year among the ghostly dead
  To Erebus' dark shadows she must go;
Then back to earth she comes to stray in glee
For ever thro' the vales of Sicily.

HYLAS

Great Heracles was lord of limb and might.
A merry boy was master of his heart:
His name was Hylas, whom the hero lov'd
With a great love of noble purity.
Winsome was his beauty as the light
That streams from off the very throne of Zeus;
His hair as sunbeams; and his eyes as blue
As the soft waters of the Midland Sea
That shine beneath the star-light and the moon;
His lips as rich in beauty as the line
Of tender, chasten'd flame, that mounts and makes
Olympus shrouded in a veil of fire.
Ever were they together, morn and night,
And thro' the long hot day; and Heracles
Taught the fair youth all prowess and delight
In manly deeds of arms and venery.
So he could box and wrestle with the boys
Of his own age and beat them, with the skill
That he had learn'd of Heracles; and swim
Thro' the cool waters of the mountain pools
Swifter than they; and chase the soft-ear'd hare
With feet as light and nimble as a hound,
Or dapple-breasted fawn; so gay was he.
And he was lov'd and honour'd by the boys
Who own'd him as their leader in all games
Of woodland skill and daring; and the girls

Eyed him with blushes, and all lov'd him well.
But he lov'd Heracles, and oft with him
Roam'd thro' the silent passes of the hills
In purest love and highest happiness
That mortal souls may know.
And when the good ship Argo started forth
With bright-ey'd Jason and the heroes all
To fetch the Golden Fleece, and Heracles
Sailed with them, Hylas followed; and the life
Of all the ship was he; and when the toil
And hardships of the voyage overweighed
The hearts of doughty heroes with the thought
That they should see their country nevermore,
Nevermore see the blue hills in the sun,
Or hear the voices of the Grecian girls
Laughing in merry welcome, then the boy
Hylas bore up their heavy hearts with song
Sweeter than any sky-lark's, in the spring,
That circles to the sun. And now at length
To the Propontine shores the heroes come,
And stop to rest and fresh their limbs awhile
After their weary rowing; for the way
Was long and full of danger and distress.
The rocks were green with mosses and the turf
Softer than any bed of down, and there
They lay and slept, and dream'd of the fair land
Whence they had come, and of the noble prize
To which they went: and on the morrow morn
Rose up renewed in strength of heart and limb
To face the sea again; yet ere they sail'd

They stay'd for one last meal on the firm land,
And to refill their cruses from the springs
That bubbled soft and fresh within the woods
Girding the quiet shore; and Heracles
Apart with Hylas sat and Telamon,
The steadfast hero and the lovely boy,
To take his meal; but Hylas soon uprose
And fetch'd his pitcher from the ship and went
Off to a little pool within the woods
That bubbled with fresh water cool and clear,
That Heracles might drink and 'suage his thirst,
And live again rejoicing in his strength.
Slowly he went his way, and on a pipe
Blowing a merry air of youth and glee;
Heracles watch'd his going, and a smile
Of pleasure in his beauty lit his face
With happiness and love. And now the boy
To the green margin of the pool is come,
Green with all tender growths and gay with flowers
That mirror back the sun, and to the pool
His pitcher now he dips, and stooping low
Watches the water sparkle as it fills
With a deep gulping sound; when suddenly
From the still water at his very feet
He sees a fairy form rise up, and then
Another and another till the pool
Is fill'd with laughing Naiads; all about
His feet they play and blush with rosiness;
Bright, radiant forms of youth, and beauteous
As anything in earth or heaven above.

They wind their soft white arms about his neck,
And kiss his ruddy lips, and bear him down,
Down to their sandy palace far beneath
The glittering water: for his beauty rare
Had stol'n their hearts; and nevermore could they
Lose sight of him again. But Hylas, he
Cried bitterly and struggled in their arms,
For he, poor boy, was loth to leave the sun
And the free sky and air, and Heracles
And all the hero band; but nought avail
His piteous cries; alone for answer came
The ripple of the water overhead,
Stirr'd by the breeze, and softly splash'd across
The rocks that lay beside the clear pool's rim
Half hidden in the rushes and the sedge.
And now the water-nymphs have borne him down,
Down in their white arms to the depths below.
And now they seek to comfort him, in vain;
All, all in vain; his tears and bitter cries
For help avail not, for they only rise
As plaintive whispers to the upper air.
But Heracles had miss'd the boy and comes
To seek him thro' the woodlands; but in vain
He shouts his name, for only echoes come.
'Hylas' he cries, and only 'Hylas' comes,
An empty voice to mock him where he stands.
Then over hill and vale the hero goes
Crying aloud; but only to his ear
The sound of the soft trickling water comes
To answer his despair. Oh nevermore

Those happy lovers there shall meet again.
Then all the heroes mourn'd for Hylas lost.
But the good Argo longs to be away,
Nor may they longer stay; but on again,
On to the toil and glory of the quest
That they have sworn to seek. But Heracles
Passes alone in sadness and dismay,
Over the desolate shore and on alone.
Nor heeds he in his grief the world around,
Hunger, or thirst, or pain; but comes, at last,
After long toils, and many a weary day,
To the wide Phasis and the far Colchian shore.

THE FOUNTAIN OF YOUTH

In Tenebros above the purple seas,
Upon a throne of beryl and of pearl,
High in a mount whose brow pierced to the stars
Sat Solomon, the Wisdom of the world,
The Prince of Men, and all about him lay
His Kingdom, the far reaches of the Earth.
Pillar and pinnacle and tow'r and town
Stretch'd to the sky's pale margin, many a plain
Travers'd by cattle and a thousand flocks
Lay there beneath the dawn; for he was lord
Of Earth and mortal creatures, birds and flow'rs,
Fish of the sea, beasts of the forest, all
Held him for ruler and his voice obey'd,
From that dread hour when in the still midnight
God had held up the balances of fate
Before his dreamy eyes, wherein he saw
On this side all the wealth of Earth's desire,
Riches and length of days and pow'r and fame,
And all of worldly glory; and on that,
Like to a single gem of costliest price,
Outweighing all, eternal wisdom lay;
Whose light alone can pierce beyond the world
And taste on earth the blessedness of heaven.
Then Solomon chose wisdom, and for this,
Since neither human joys nor gloried fame
Enticed his heart, the Lord of Heaven decreed
These also should be added unto him.
So kingly now he sat and ruled the world,

While round him rolled the panoply of heaven,
White mist and floating vapours gossamer
In wreaths of cloud majestic; but his throne
Shone with the purple splendour of a dawn
In high midsummer; for whose canopy
Tendrils of creeping plants and languorous flow'rs
Wove a cool bow'r upon the mountain side:
Frail honeysuckle and pink eglantine
And Posidonian roses drenched with dew,
Where all around a radiant galaxy
Of youthful forms, glowing with slender grace,
Shone like pale stars across a summer night;
And many an ancient sage and warrior scarr'd
Stood round their lord in counsel, while above,
His merry-throated courtiers of the sky
Offered their praise of ceaseless symphony.

Then thro' the haze that heralded the splendour
Of the triumphant pageant of the sun,
Riding in golden glory o'er the earth,
Father of life and lord of hearts that kindle
With the deep fire of love, there broke to sight,
Sudden and awful like a cloud of fear
That breaks upon a heedless merriment,
A phantom hand whose fingers bore aloft
A chalice of cool jasper, wherein flamed
Deep lustrous wine as crimson as the lips
Of young Adonis; clearer than the dew,
And fragrant as the passion-kindled breath
Of youthful lovers kissing like twin flow'rs

Thro' all a summer night; so sweet it rose
Upon the mountain air, till all the throng
That smelt its beauty felt their drowsy hearts
Wake to such life each pulse was ecstasy:
While tender music seemed to fill their ears
Till all their being throbb'd to wondrous love
That knew not baseness nor impure desire.
Then from the mist an airy voice uprose
In song that dazed the echoes with delight;
In tones as softly precious as the shower
Of crystal music springing from the lips
Of some fresh-throated singing-boy, whose praise
Soars to the rafters of a chapel bow'r,
In rich unclouded beauty, till the heart
Sinks into dreams of rapture; so the burden
Trailed now upon the summer-honey'd air,
In accents magical—'To thee, great King,
From the dread Warden of the world I bring
This precious cup and still more precious potion
Fairer than wine, more mighty than old ocean
To work man weal or sorrow; if in truth
Thy heart desireth an eternal youth
Of strength and joy and love's soft ravishment,
Of supple grace and beauty's blandishment—
If thou dost yearn for an immortal Spring,
Flowers that fade not, birds that ever sing,
Lift this enchanted beaker to thy lips,
Sweet is its savour and whoever sips
Never shall feel his joyous life decay,
But heaven shall crown him with immortal day,

Still shall he feel his blood kindle and glow
With love's warm dalliance; still his spirits flow
In floods of rapturous music at the thrill
Of youthful beauty, and his being fill
With all the tender yearnings of desire,
With all the heat of passion's restless fire;
For tho' the forms he cherish pass away,
New loves shall spring like blossoms of the May
For each succeeding year; the choice is thine—
Drink for thy pleasure and no more repine
At thoughts of passing life, and the dark night,
Whose shades up-gather that must quench delight,
And hide the beauty that thine eyes adore
In clouds of darkling sorrow evermore.'
So sang the voice and ceased, and sound was still.
Then Solomon sighed deeply, for the choice,
True love and death, life and the passing light
Of fleeting whims, lay heavy at his heart.
So sweet the morn! so dear the leaping tide
Of days that sweep life with them to the sea
Whence no belated mariner returns
To breathe a murmur of the lonely shore
In eager ears that mourn for lost delight!
So sweet the pomp, so glorious the power,
To rule in splendour over hosts of men
That answer to his sway; and still the doubt—
'True-love may die beyond the bourn of death,'
Throbs ever at the portals of his brain,
Seeking for entrance, and what then avail
The troth and faith of lovers, if the dead

Feel not the glow of beauty, nor can hear
The precious music of fulfilled desire?

Then took he counsel of the sons of men,
And all the mortal children of the earth,
That still must die and perish, still must see
The lovely hues of beauty pale anon
To bloodless age, and passionate limbs decay
From strength and grace, to weakness, and the slow
Living corruption, mocking in its sadness
The ghastly face of death, and the dark tomb.

Then spake those hollow servitors whose lips
Echo but flattery and ignoble thoughts—
That think not of true counsel nor the words
Of guileless friendship, but of their own ends,
Which they to serve strive ever, yet would seem
But offering still the tribute of their love—
'Yea, drink, dear lord,' they cry, 'for not alone
Hangeth thy fate upon the solemn choice,
Fear for the passing of thy glorious life
All nature and all races doth dismay:
For who like thee can sway the peopled earth,
Who shall arise to grasp with mighty hand
Thy sov'reign sceptre, thy imperial crown?
Nay, drink, dear lord, nor fear the charméd cup,
'Tis but a presage from the eternal God
To try thee if thy heart repineth now:
If all the care and labour of the world,
And loss of friends, and the sore wounds of love,

Wrenched from thy sorrowing heart by greedy Death,
Can tempt thee to forgo thy furnished power,
And reign of His vicegerent upon Earth ;
Can draw thy heart away from that high trust
Thy God bestoweth ever upon thee,
With dreams of quiet and obscure repose,
To seek a paradise of idle rest.'

Thus said they all, yet had their specious words
No power to beguile their wary king;
He saw the cautious mockery of their hearts
And double-speechèd tongues, and could descry
Beneath their open counsel and loud praise,
The laughter of their self-encumbered souls.

Next spake the preying beasts whose hearts obey
Nought but high Wisdom and her master, Love;
No fear they knew of Solomon, for he,
Alone of mortal beings, could discern
The secrets of their souls; alone could read
The darkness of their passion and their pain,
And draw them with love's fetters to himself
Out of the mists and perils of that life
God had ordainèd for them; and could soothe
Their querulous moods and passionate, fierce breasts
To gentleness and trust, and bid dismay
Be absent at their coming among men.
So calm they came as servants to his hest
And licked with docile tongues his outstretch'd hands,
To pay their homage to the king of earth,
Ready to do his bidding, and obey

The teachings of his mouth, with that shy rev'rence
Of turbulent creatures tamed to human pow'r;
And all the pathos of their lonely pride,
And all the wonder of their glorious strength,
Spake to the wistful heart of Solomon.
For these were children of the Prince of Heaven,
Living to praise him after their desire
With all the beauty of their supple limbs
And restless woodland grace, and tenderness
For their young, helpless offspring: to fulfil
Their ordered life; and tread the paths none fixed
But the all-seeing eye and burning breast
Alone of that unfathomable Love.
Then spake they each to Solomon their king—
The crested lion in his lowering pride,
The tiger with her cunning, pard and bear,
And solemn elephant, and wolf and ape,
And all the fierce-eyed strangers of the wild,
Gave counsel to their Sov'reign in his hour
Of gloom and doubt, and dark perplexity.
Yet, for the bonds that drew them were not wrought
Of Reason but the braided strands of Love,
Their speech came from the chambers of the heart
That brooks not cession of the thing beloved,
And thus they also counselled him to drink
Of the distilled enchantment, that could yield—
If the veil'd voice spake truth—undying life
On the familiar earth; with all its deeps
Of joy, and the quick pulse of dear desire,
Yearning to be fulfilled with love's intent.

So spake they, and again the illumined eye
Of Solomon, lit with ineffable
Clear radiancy of wisdom, viewed their minds,
And read the pathos of their simple trust.
And fiercer yet the dark enticement came,
For now the doubt shot over the still deeps
Of reason whether verily the choice
Were proffered him of God or that fell power
That striveth e'er for man's allegiance.

Then lastly called he to him from the depths
Of a great forest where the sun's masked fire
Slants chastenedly across the lonely glades,
His aery agent, Bontimar the dove,
Faithful thro' years of quiet confidence,
By gentle life proved seemly and sedate
To weigh a matter and adjust the scale,
And strike a balance between heart and soul:
But Bontimar flew sadly to her lord
Knowing the truth and gauging in its light
The strife of spirit for the victory;
And all the weary combat of the heart
'Twixt present gladness and the uncertain gloom
That flits so fitfully o'er the hills of death.
And sorrowfully she spake as if in fear
Lest all the earthly glamour should prevail
Against her single rede, lest at the last
The heavenly seed might perish, lest the tares
That choked it, for true fruit be garnered in.
'Master,' she softly spake—'though joy is dear,

And for man's life as the clear sparkling wine,
Gladding the heart and lifting up the soul
From its frail diaphane of petulant flesh,
Yet whence doth flow this liquor of delight?
From what full-swelling grapes, from what sweet vines,
That trellis the fair hills of heart's desire,
Do such founts spring? Love is alone the source
Of that deep magic wine of joy, for Love
Swelleth beneath the sunny hours of life,
Clinging with burning tendrils to that vine
Whose leaves are beauty and whose branches grace:
And love, true love, no years can bring again
Strong as the bands that bind the heart of youth,
When life is grace, and beauty is desire;
For thou hast known the mantling of the cheek,
And all the blissful sorrow that attends
The first full rush of love; the secret speech
Eyes teach each other, and the deep content
Born of that precious madness of delight
When lips of love seek beauty from thy own.
Then wish not the dull years of deathless life,
While all that made life sweetest must decay
And draw beyond the impenetrable shade
That masketh pleasure from the eyes of light.
Thou hast drunk deeply of the wine of love,
Drink not then of this other, but await
(Tho' the long years yield sadness, and tho' fear
Grippeth the bravest at the touch of doom)
That silent last adventure, that shall bring
Thee with thy dearest to the glades of peace,

Where joy undying reigneth evermore.'

Thus spake she and grew silent, for her tongue
Reck'd nought of eloquence, but spelt alone
Her sweet untunéd singleness of heart.
And Solomon perceived the charity
And blessing of his simple counsellor,
Who sought not honey'd sentences, but framed
Rude words to clothe the naked truths that throng'd
Blunt and ill-pleasing thro' her patient soul;
And all the dear illusions vanishéd
That he had sought to bind about his sight,
And now again the beams of wisdom shone
Scorning the mists of vanity and care
For soft inglorious ease and dull content;
And all the love that smoulder'd in his soul
Broke to fierce flame that rankled and consumed
The pyre of dark inanity within.
Then sorrowfully he spake, as feeling yet
The sway of mortal pleasure, tho' his will
Bowed as a vassal before Wisdom's throne,
'O Bontimar, thou hast conquer'd, for my heart
Rings with true music that thy words set free,
There is for all a fearsome way to tread
Thro' the dark distance, where no radiancy
Shines on the path we traverse from the known
Lost borders of the dear familiar land
Whence we set out, nor any beacon light
Glows to clear triumph from the land of joy
Our spirits yearn to dwell in; and for this,

We clutch at the last strands that bind our life
To mortal dwellings, and the sweet caress
Of friendly wayfarers whose ears as yet
Hear not the heavenly summons; yet for truth
We snatch at empty phantoms that impede
Our passage to the long eternal home:
There shall we know the plenitude of love,
There taste its perfect rapture, and receive
The key that frees the secrets of desire.
Take then, O mystic voice, thy answer now.
Not for eternal youth and all the pride
Of earthly pomp and glory, I forgo
The boon of death that maketh ever new
The hearts of mortals; that alone can quench
Their burning thirst for beauty and delight
In the fresh fount of everlasting Love.'

He ceased, and on the sullen air there fell
A deep and pregnant veil of quietness:
Into the haze the flaming cup withdrew,
And the mist trembled into tenuous day.

THE SOUTHERN POLE

Video meliora proboque, deteriora sequor. (Ovid.)

I

Ye climes of frozen silence and still deeps!
Ye wastes of voiceless waters armour'd o'er
With crystal, for a path from shore to shore!
And you ye snowy steeps!
Voices of ageless mystery and fear
Whisper your secret to the echoing wind,
Moaning and wailing as it travels on
To realms more smiled on by the blessed sun,
To lands that bear the mark of human kind,
From ways forlorn and desolation drear.

II

Thro' the long vigil of the dawnless night,
Thro' the pale twilight of the eveless day,
Wardens of solitude! ye hold your sway
Far from all human sight.
Your kingdoms of sad silence and pale gloom
Rul'd by no human powers the years pursue;
Your subjects are the strange sea-monster's brood,
Half fish, half beast, of loathly form endued,
And glossy seals with skins of silvery hue
That make the ice their lair, the sea their tomb.

III

What far-off, echoing, syren-voices call?
  What soft enchantment do your breezes blow?
What deathly lures, what harbingers of woe
  Our human hearts enthral?
Doth some live murmur touch our spirits still,
  Some long-forgotten human memory,
From the far ages of man's early birth,
  When frozen glooms cover'd the fruitful earth,
While towering ice-bergs sailed our English sea,
  And the snows thickened upon crag and hill?

IV

For still some strange irrefutable spell
  Draws human footsteps to your dreary shore!
Thro' weary labour and privation sore
  The lonely hours they tell,
Who far away from haunt of human-kind,
  The loves they cherish and the homes they prize,
To that bleak barren world of silence go,
  Where, for their homeland, lies the eternal snow,
For friendly welcome, but the cheerless skies:
  What guerdon meetly glorious can they find?

V

O Wisdom, glorious mistress of the soul!
  And of such children doubly justified,
For thee they live; thy glory all their pride,
  Who to no fruitless goal
Press on in spite of hazard and distress,
  Of numbing peril and of dread alarm,
To lay so rich a trophy at thy feet.
  For thee they face the blinding blizzard's sleet,
For thee they seek the laurel and the palm,
  And toil to feed thy flame thro' weariness.

VI

And we whose life is wayward, whom shy Hope
  Never hath lured across the trackless sea,
In some great emprise of high chivalry,
  We who but blindly grope,
Till dull Convention's gloom our souls enslave,
  Shot with no mystic visions of romance;
Who follow the safe track our Fathers wore,
  Nor feel the thirst to drink dark Wisdom's lore
In some uncharted fairyland of Chance,
  What guerdon do we carry to the grave?

VII

Too often but the memory of life
  Ill-spent, ill-founded ; with no certain goal
To tempt with nobler dreams the unstrung soul ;
  And thoughts of fruitless strife—
Of battle with our friends instead of foes
  For worthless trophies and ill-placed desires,
'Midst cries of pain unheeded and forlorn.
  And for this heritage our souls were born ?—
To cringe and perish in these treacherous fires ?
  Or win thro' blood and flame our heart's repose ?

VIII

Yet still, Imperious Goddess, is thy throne
  Set up on pedestals of fallen men,
Who in the long march drop from human ken
  To find their rest alone :
In thy proud service stricken mortally,
  Yet glorying in the battle and the pain ;
Willing in such dear emprise to be sped,
  If so the lamp of Wisdom may be fed,
And by their deeds flicker to life again ;
  Then gladly would they droop to earth and die.

IX

And thus to purge our listless, fever'd way,
  Comes like a tonic show'r the glorious tale
(Truly the springs of Manhood shall not fail
  While earth breeds such as they!)
Of that proud band of heroes and their prize
  Of aching toil and martyr victory,
Of pain endured in silence, till life's breath
  Falter'd and failed before remorseless Death,
Then one by one they laid them down to die
  And he, their Captain, clos'd the frozen eyes.

X

Then he too fared on that eternal quest,
  On man's last, great adventurous voyage to go,
Far out upon the senseless wastes of snow,
  Still with the same high zest
As e'er had marked his hours of mortal breath;
  Fearless, nor sad, for in his soul there shone
The steadfast Lamp of Truth, and in its light
  Bravely he gat him out into the night
To face Time's last and fellest Champion,
  And silence lorded o'er the Camp of Death.

XI

And what of him, their comrade who alone
   Marched out to meet that silent Conqueror,
If haply by his death he might restore
   Lives loved above his own?
Shall his proud name die with the dying years?
   O rather shall his praise for ever ring
Adown the ages for such Chivalry:
   While men shall live his memory shall not die,
His deed the lips of bards unborn shall sing
   And that proud fate bewail with mournful tears

XII

What went they forth to seek, and what to find?
   The tribute of pure fame for noble deed?
Alas! a colder token was their meed,
   Snow-wreaths their temples bind.
The praise for worlds new-born to men? or yet,
   The knowledge of far lands their feet alone
Of human limbs had trod since Time began?
   But other feet their luckless steps outran,
O'er that drear waste another flag had flown:
   Yet praise, with heroes, triumphs o'er regret.

XIII

And yet I know they shall not wholly die,
Still in the living memory of Time,
Unchanged, undimmed, unchallenged, but sublime
Their fame eternally
Shall spread from out the fastness of their rest;
Not first nor chiefly of their triumphs won,
Of new-found knowledge or their hapless doom,
Of deathly perils and the lonely tomb;
But rather for heroic service done,
Praise of all praise the noblest and the best.

XIV

Weep not nor mourn for heroes that are dead,
But rather, as Laconian mothers, sing
A paean for their glory's heightening;
Their Spirit is not shed,
But lives and stirs thro' all our human ways,
And shall live ever while the earth may be
A human dwelling place: their lustrous fame
Time shall not pale. The splendour of their name
Thrills round the glorious earth from sea to sea
In one loud concert of triumphant praise.

Printed in the United States
By Bookmasters